Presented To

_____

Presented By

_____

Date

PROVERBS
FOR LIFE
for *You*

Ψ
inspirio™

Proverbs for Life™ for You
ISBN 0-310-80180-X

Copyright 2003 by GRQ Ink, Inc.
Franklin, Tennessee 37067

"Proverbs for Life" is a trademark owned by GRQ, Inc.

Published by Inspirio™, The gift group of Zondervan
5300 Patterson Avenue, SE
Grand Rapids, Michigan 49530

Requests for information should be addressed to:
Inspirio™, The gift group of Zondervan
Grand Rapids, Michigan 49530
http://www.inspiriogifts.com

Compiler: Lila Empson
Associate Editor: Janice Jacobson
Project Manager: Tom Dean
Manuscript written by Michael J. Foster in conjunction with
   Snapdragon Editorial Group, Inc.
Design: Whisner Design Group

02 03 04/HK/ 4 3 2 1

Do yourself a favor and

learn all you can;

then remember what you learn

and you will prosper.

Proverbs 19:8 gnt

Contents

Introduction

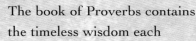

The book of Proverbs contains the timeless wisdom each person needs to live a happy, healthy, well balanced life—each entry teaching a practical principle designed to encourage good choices and positive problem solving.

Proverbs for Life™ for You takes those valuable principles and applies them to the issues you care about most—such as family, health, peace, and commitment. As you read through these pages, may you find the practical answers—God's answers—to the questions you are asking.

Reverence for the LORD is an education in itself.

— *Proverbs 15:33 GNT*

God's Majesty

My God, how wonderful Thou art!
Thy majesty how bright!
How beautiful Thy mercy-seat,
In depths of burning light!
How wonderful, how beautiful,
The sight of Thee must be,
Thine endless wisdom, boundless power,
And aweful purity!

Frederick William Faber

The Gift of Time

A man's wisdom gives him patience; it is to his glory to overlook an offense.

~ *Proverbs 19:11 NIV*

At the time, Glenda felt it was the right thing to do—opening her home to Neva and the boys until she could get back on her feet. That's what a sister's supposed to do, right?

Glenda thought Neva would find her own place quickly, but she hadn't shown much interest in looking. Now things were getting tense. Glenda loved her sister, but each day it seemed there was some fresh intrusion, some new inconvenience, another misunderstanding.

"Lord, help me to be patient," Glenda prayed. "Give me the strength to see Neva through this difficult time."

Ten days later, Neva excitedly announced she had found an apartment. They would be moving soon.

"You've given me more than a place to stay," she told Glenda. "You've given me the gift of time. Time to decide what kind of life I really want. Time to think about my options. Time to ask for God's help. Thanks, Sis."

Your natural store of patience is based solely on what you see and hear—surface material. That's why it sometimes runs out when people don't respond in the way you feel is appropriate. But God sees through all the circumstances, behaviors, and personality issues. He sees straight into the heart, and therefore, his patience is always deeper than your own. The good news is that if you ask him, he will impart to you the patience you need to fulfill his purposes. Do you need more patience?

TRY THIS: *Draw a small heart on a piece of paper. Each time your patience with a particular person or situation is tested, draw a slightly larger heart on top of the first, asking God to increase your patience by increasing your love. Then watch for the miracles—one in your heart and one in the other person's life.*

BE COMPLETELY HUMBLE AND GENTLE; BE PATIENT, BEARING WITH ONE ANOTHER IN LOVE.

EPHESIANS 4:2 NIV

IT IS BETTER TO BE PATIENT THAN POWERFUL. IT IS BETTER TO WIN CONTROL OVER YOURSELF THAN OVER WHOLE CITIES.

PROVERBS 16:32 GNT

Faith takes up the cross, love binds it to the soul, patience bears it to the end.

HORATIUS BONAR

SLEEPING WELL

Who can say, "I have kept my heart pure; I am clean and without sin"?

~ *Proverbs* 20:9 NIV

A BAD
CONSCIENCE
EMBITTERS THE
SWEETEST
COMFORTS;
A GOOD
CONSCIENCE
SWEETENS THE
BITTEREST
CROSSES.
—WENDELL PHILLIPS

Daniel was a good person. He always did the right thing when it came to the obvious—he wouldn't have considered cheating on his taxes, stealing from his employer, or telling a lie. It was the gray area that seemed to confuse him and leave him staring at the ceiling into the late hours—like tonight.

It hadn't seemed like a big deal at first—listening in on his boss's personal discussion with a coworker. But now, the nagging, unsettled feeling in the pit of his stomach was saying it was a big deal. Closing his eyes, he asked God to forgive him for violating his coworker's privacy and his own integrity.

"Lord, show me how to make this right," he prayed. "And thank you for the nudging of your Spirit deep inside."

It's impossible to overestimate the importance of a clear conscience. Ignoring that nagging feeling deep within can rob you of your sleep, your sense of peace and well-being, and your relationships. It's good to know that God has provided a remedy. He has promised to forgive you and restore your peace—as long as you are faithful to respond to your conscience by taking responsibility for your wrong actions and asking for his help.

Try this: Most Bibles have topical indexes. After clearing your conscience by asking God to forgive you, look in your Bible for a verse that applies to your wrongful action or thought—such as Proverbs 12:19 for honesty. Then read the verse out loud each night before you go to bed for at least one week and ask God to instill the principle in your heart.

LET US DRAW NEAR TO GOD WITH A SINCERE HEART IN FULL ASSURANCE OF FAITH, HAVING OUR HEARTS SPRINKLED TO CLEANSE US FROM A GUILTY CONSCIENCE.

HEBREWS 10:22 NIV

KEEP YOUR FAITH AND A CLEAR CONSCIENCE.

1 TIMOTHY 1:19 GNT

Labor to keep alive in your breast that little spark of celestial fire called conscience.

GEORGE WASHINGTON

A Better Way

The righteousness of the upright delivers them, but the unfaithful are trapped by evil desires.

— *Proverbs* 11:6 NIV

INTEGRITY IS THE FIRST STEP TO TRUE GREATNESS.
—CHARLES SIMMONS

When Jean went back to college after years away from the world of academia, she soon realized that juggling personal responsibilities and a long list of class assignments left her exhausted and struggling. No wonder she perked up when a classmate told her about an Internet site that supplied essays and term papers for a fee.

Late one evening, Jean went so far as to visit the site. But as she sat there staring at the screen, she knew in her heart that cheating was not the solution to her dilemma.

Instead, she asked God to help her make better use of the time she had. As always, he was faithful to show her ways to keep her head above water. It was a tough semester, but Jean was glad she had chosen to navigate the course with her integrity intact.

It's tempting to allow a lapse in your personal integrity when you're out of time and feeling the stress of all your commitments. But unethical shortcuts—cheating, being dishonest, taking advantage of others—just aren't worth it. They draw you in and trap you in a cycle of compromise, robbing you of your sense of fulfillment. If you are willing to ask, God is able to help you find an honorable way to deal with any situation or circumstance.

Try this: Adopt the twenty-four-hour rule. Consider your proposed solution to a particular challenge for twenty-four hours. Use that time to think about the possible consequences. If it threatens to compromise your personal integrity, the price is too high. Ask God to help you find an alternative answer, one that won't cost you more than you can afford to pay.

He who walks in integrity walks securely.

Proverbs 10:9 NASB

The integrity of the upright will guide them.

Proverbs 11:3 NASB

Knowledge without integrity is dangerous and dreadful.

Samuel Johnson

15

Is He My Brother?

Be generous, and you will be prosperous.
Help others, and you will be helped.

— *Proverbs 11:25* GNT

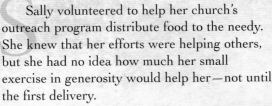

GOD HAS GIVEN
US TWO HANDS—
ONE FOR
RECEIVING AND
THE OTHER FOR
GIVING.
—BILLY GRAHAM

Sally volunteered to help her church's outreach program distribute food to the needy. She knew that her efforts were helping others, but she had no idea how much her small exercise in generosity would help her—not until the first delivery.

When the old church van pulled to a stop in front of a small house that morning, Sally and another volunteer carried boxes of assorted canned goods to the front door. As they climbed the steps to the porch, the screen door opened. A pregnant woman and two small children stood in the doorway with big smiles.

For the next twenty minutes, Sally played with the kids and helped shelve the food in the family's empty pantry. As she and the other volunteer drove away toward their next stop, Sally waved good-bye and thought that for the first time in a long time, she felt full inside. By giving just a little of her time and effort, she had received nourishment for that empty place in her heart.

There are many ways to exercise generosity. You may have more time than money, more belongings than time. Whatever abundance God has blessed you with, share it with others. In that way, you will be fulfilling God's desire for each of us—to love and care for those around us. Don't let your heart become a stagnant pond. As God's blessings flow in, open the doors and let them flow out to others. You will find that in giving, you become richer.

Try this: Find out which food items your local church or food bank needs. Go grocery shopping as you always do, but the next time you find incredible deals, buy more than you can use and donate the surplus. Don't be content with giving the unwanted food from the back of your cupboard. Rather, be blessed by sharing your abundance.

He who gives to the poor will lack nothing.

Proverbs 28:27 NIV

Be generous and share your food with the poor. You will be blessed for it.

Proverbs 22:9 GNT

You do not have to be rich to be generous. If he has the spirit of true generosity, a pauper can give like a prince.

Corrine U. Wells

God's Blessing

Things that Count

Not what we have, but what we use;

Not what we see, but what we choose.

These are the things that mar or bless

The sum of human happiness.

Not what we take, but what we give;

Not as we pray, but as we live,

These are the things that make for peace,

Both now and after time shall cease.

Author Unknown

The blessing of the
LORD brings wealth, and
he adds no trouble to it.

— *Proverbs* 10:22 NIV

The Lord said, "I will
send down showers in
season; there will be
showers of blessing."

— *Ezekiel* 34:26 NIV

BLESSINGS EVER

WAIT ON VIRTUOUS

DEEDS.

ENGLISH PROVERB

A Simple Prayer

He who gets wisdom loves his own soul; he who cherishes understanding prospers.

— Proverbs 19:8 NIV

Greg desperately needed a better car. The one he had leaked oil and was rusting away. Wandering through the lots at the auto dealers, he noted all the choices from sport coupes to pickup trucks. The trouble was, Greg wasn't sure what he was looking for. All he knew was what his budget could afford.

When Greg got home, he thought about all the cars he had seen and driven. He felt confused. Greg decided to sleep on it. Before going to bed, Greg prayed and asked God to help him make sense of everything.

The next morning, Greg woke refreshed—a car that he had seen, but not driven, nudged his consciousness. Heading back to the dealership for a better look, he noted that the car was attractive and in great shape. This was the one! Using his old car as a trade-in, Greg was able to negotiate a reasonable price.

Wisdom is the art of taking the information you have and making good choices. That may not sound tough, but it often is. That's why God says if you need wisdom, you should just ask for it and he will give it to you freely. He won't do the legwork for you, but he will sure help you see through the fog of emotional sales pitches and conflicting considerations. As a kind and loving father, he wants you to make good choices.

Try this: *Start a wisdom journal. Every night list one important decision you made during the day. In addition, explain why that decision was ultimately wise or unwise. The next time you are struggling with a tough decision, browse through your wisdom journal. Your documented experiences can be a valuable resource in assisting you with your decision-making process.*

HAPPY IS ANYONE WHO BECOMES WISE—WHO COMES TO HAVE UNDERSTANDING.

PROVERBS 3:13 GNT

IF ANY OF YOU LACKS WISDOM, HE SHOULD ASK GOD, WHO GIVES GENEROUSLY TO ALL WITHOUT FINDING FAULT.

JAMES 1:5 NIV

God grant me the serenity to accept things I cannot change, courage to change things I can, and wisdom to know the difference.

REINHOLD NIEBUHR

Lead Me, Lord!

For lack of guidance a nation falls, but many advisers make victory sure.

— *Proverbs 11:14 NIV*

SURROUND YOURSELF WITH THE BEST PEOPLE YOU CAN FIND.
—RONALD REAGAN

It was a hard-fought campaign, but John Campbell and his supporters had won the election by a slim margin. John knew it was time to begin what he was determined to do—make a difference.

John's first act as city councilman was to pray for wisdom in selecting his group of personal advisors. As important city issues would be debated, John knew that he would receive God-honored advice from these advisors.

The Reverend Parker, John's pastor, frequently reminded him of his responsibilities as a Christian, and Dr. Adams, his college English professor, helped him write his speeches. Judge Evans provided valuable counsel on legal issues and timeless wisdom, while his best friend, Kyle, offered down-to-earth practical advice that was rooted in scripture. Most important, however, was John's reliance on God. John understood that God had been with him every step of the way, and that no matter how difficult the dilemma, his decisions would be tempered with experience, thoughtfulness, and insight.

In your life, do you feel that you have to help yourself? Do you feel you must rely on your own abilities and understanding? God wants you to rely on him and his understanding. Not only will he help you to seek out and find wise advisors who can provide wisdom and guidance, but he will personally help you by showing you your motives and those of others, leading you in the right direction at the right time, and giving you a sense of confidence in what you are doing.

Try this: *Assemble your own "panel of advisors." Write down five names of people that you admire and why you trust them. When you pray, ask God to bless them and fill them with wisdom. Whenever you feel you are in need of guidance, pray first, and then seek advice from someone on your panel of advisors.*

I guide you in the way of wisdom and lead you along straight paths.

Proverbs 4:11 NIV

Wise men store up knowledge.

Proverbs 10:14 NIV

He that won't be counseled can't be helped.

Benjamin Franklin

All I Need

*The fear of the LORD leads to life: then one rests content,
untouched by trouble.*

~ *Proverbs 19:23* NIV

Content makes
poor men rich;
discontent
makes rich men
poor.
—Benjamin
Franklin

The fire had destroyed the Johnsons' home and all their possessions. It had left them feeling as if they had lost themselves. Stripped of their belongings, however, they each made an important discovery: their possessions didn't define who they were—God did.

Seeing how quickly their possessions could go up in smoke left them unwilling to continue their futile pursuit of things. They settled into a more comfortable way of life, one where they placed more value on the things that last, like their relationships with God and with each other.

The Johnsons soon found a new joy in their lives—the joy that comes with a lack of striving. As they replaced their possessions, they also put their priorities in order. For each chair and bed and plate, they thanked God for the lasting things that could not be destroyed. They had lost a great deal but found something far more valuable—contentment.

Do you appreciate who you are and what you have? Or are you continually striving for more things and more status and more accomplishments, no matter how much you already have? Do you find that you are never satisfied with your life? God knows that a life filled with striving will only lead to frustration and burn out. He promises that when you release your intense desires to him, he will fill you instead with a satisfying sense of contentment and joy.

TRY THIS: *Create a blessings list. Begin with five items and hang it in a place in your home or office where you will see it every day. Each day add at least one new item to the list. When the first page is full, add a second page over the top of it. Once a month, read back over your list.*

GIVE ME NEITHER POVERTY NOR RICHES, BUT GIVE ME ONLY MY DAILY BREAD.

PROVERBS 30:8 NIV

KEEP YOUR LIVES FREE FROM THE LOVE OF MONEY, AND BE SATISFIED WITH WHAT YOU HAVE.

HEBREWS 13:5 GNT

Contentment is a pearl of great price, and whoever procures it at the expense of ten thousand desires makes a wise and a happy purchase.

JOHN BALGUY

I'll Do Better Next Time

A soft answer turneth away wrath: but grievous words stir up anger.

~ *Proverbs 15:1 KJV*

ANGER IS
QUIETED BY A
GENTLE WORD
JUST AS FIRE IS
QUENCHED BY
WATER.
—JEAN PIERRE
CAMUS

Emily gasped when she saw the big purple stain on the carpet, and the nearby white guest towel was also stained. What was it—grape juice? She could feel her blood pressure rising and angry words forming. Then she looked up and saw her six-year-old daughter, Cassie, standing quietly beside her.

"I'm sorry, Mom," she began meekly. "I spilled my juice, and when I saw the big purple spot on the rug, I got scared. I thought you would be so mad. I tried to wipe it up. Now the towel is ruined and the carpet is still a mess." Cassie began to cry.

Emily's angry words stuck in her throat as she put her arms around her daughter. Cassie's solemn confession had pinpointed Emily's own shortcoming—angry words too often spoken in haste. "It's okay Cassie," she promised. "I'm sure it was an accident. We'll clean it up together. Next time we'll both do better."

When you feel you have been wronged and your wishes have been ignored, it's a natural response to get hot under the collar. But don't let your anger reign. Don't place yourself and those around you under its power. Surrendering your anger to God and letting him replace it with peace is a much more productive solution. If you ask, he will give you the words to express your concerns without the hurtful sting of an angry encounter. Are you practicing the power of peace?

TRY THIS: *When you feel anger rising up inside you, keep your mouth closed. Take a moment to pray and ask God to help you respond by practicing the power of peace. After you have had time to pray and consider your response, write out your concerns before verbalizing them.*

HUMAN ANGER DOES NOT ACHIEVE GOD'S RIGHTEOUS PURPOSE.

JAMES 1:20 GNT

A FOOL GIVES FULL VENT TO HIS ANGER, BUT A WISE MAN KEEPS HIMSELF UNDER CONTROL.

PROVERBS 29:11 NIV

If you are patient in one moment of anger, you will avoid one hundred days of sorrow.
ANCIENT PROVERB

GOD's COMPASSION

Tell me about the Master!
Of the wrong He freely forgave,
Of His love and tender compassion,
Of His love that is mighty to save.

For I know that whatever of sorrow,
Or pain or temptation befall,
The Infinite Master has suffered,
And knoweth and pitieth all.

AUTHOR UNKNOWN

Whoever is kind to the needy honors God.

~ *Proverbs 14:31 NIV*

The LORD is gracious and righteous; our God is full of compassion.

~ *Psalm 116:5 NIV*

MAN MAY DISMISS COMPASSION FROM HIS HEART, BUT GOD NEVER WILL.

WILLIAM COWPER

For Her Good

There is a friend who sticks closer than a brother.

~ Proverbs 18:24 NIV

Elizabeth knew that Jessica had only gone on a few dates with Scott, but she also knew that Jessica thought he was great. Scott was handsome and very funny, and Jessica enjoyed the time they spent together. This is what made it difficult for Elizabeth, who was her best friend, to tell Jessica what she knew.

Elizabeth knew Scott from work. He had a bad reputation from many interoffice romances. Elizabeth had known more than one coworker who had dated him and regretted it. She also knew he could be charming but manipulative. His infamous jealousy was made worse by a horrible temper.

Elizabeth had the difficult task of telling Jessica what she knew about him. At first, Jessica didn't believe it, or rather she didn't want to believe it. But after the next date, Elizabeth's warnings began to prove true. Before the relationship progressed any further, and before anyone could get hurt, Jessica stopped dating Scott.

Being a friend is never an easy job. It takes caring, self-sacrifice, and honesty. If you tell your friends exactly what they want to hear—as opposed to what they need to hear—you are doing them a disservice. It may be uncomfortable, but if you focus on what is best for your friends, you will never go wrong. Even though they may occasionally be offended, they will eventually be thankful for your faithfulness and might even return the favor someday.

Try this: On plain, white index cards, write "I welcome your honesty" and sign your name. Give one to each of your best friends. Ask them to always be honest with you even if it seems uncomfortable or embarrassing. Ask them if they would like you to make the same pledge to them. Then expect them to keep their promise.

WOUNDS FROM A FRIEND CAN BE TRUSTED, BUT AN ENEMY MULTIPLIES KISSES.

PROVERBS 27:6 NIV

GREATER LOVE HAS NO ONE THAN THIS, THAT HE LAY DOWN HIS LIFE FOR HIS FRIENDS.

JOHN 15:13 NIV

It is better to have one true friend than all the acquaintances in the world.

AUTHOR UNKNOWN

THE BOSS'S NEW POLICY

He who guards his mouth and his tongue keeps himself from calamity.

— *Proverbs 21:23 NIV*

Everyone was talking about the new supervisor—how they disliked the way he kept changing things. Ellen remained silent on the matter, but she understood their complaints, and sympathized with their frustration.

While in the break room, a couple of her coworkers asked, "What do you think about the boss's new policy plan to shorten our lunch break?" Of all the changes, Ellen disliked this one the most, but instead of complaining, she responded, "I'm sure that in time we will get used to it." Disappointed with her answer, the two coworkers left grumbling. As Ellen finished her soda, she looked up to see her boss standing in a nearby doorway.

"I heard what you said to the others," he said. "And I want to thank you. I know the changes I'm making are unpopular, but I do have a plan. Thanks for keeping a good attitude!"

It often feels good, even justified, to gripe and complain, but the most successful people have learned to keep their wits about them. Nothing good ever comes from speaking negatively. It's better to offer positive, encouraging words or to keep your opinions to yourself until you are in an appropriate environment for addressing certain issues. By finding the best in every situation, however small, you can minimize your frustrations and guarantee that your words will never be the cause of confusion and strife.

Try this: When you are having negative feelings about someone, write his or her name at the top of a sheet of paper. List the negative feelings you are having on one side. For every negative feeling, then list three positive things on the other side. You will find the positive input will help stabilize your attitude.

The speech of the upright rescues them.

Proverbs 12:6 NIV

Thoughtless words can wound as deeply as any sword, but wisely spoken words can heal.

Proverbs 12:18 GNT

Wisdom is knowing when to speak your mind and when to mind your speech.

Author Unknown

The Best Shop on Main Street

The tongue that brings healing is a tree of life.

— *Proverbs 15:4 NIV*

Encouragement costs you nothing to give, but it is priceless to receive.
—Author Unknown

The antique store was beautifully decorated, but surprisingly quiet. Amanda browsed through the shop and stopped to look at an old oak wardrobe.

"Are you looking for anything particular today?" asked the shop owner.

Amanda turned around and responded, "No, no. I'm just enjoying this nice day and admiring your beautiful antiques. How has business been?"

The shopkeeper shook his head and said, "It can't get much worse. It seems that business has been bad for everyone lately."

Amanda laughed, "That bad, huh? Well, it can't be for lack of trying. You have the best looking shop on Main Street. Your window displays are so beautiful. They caught my eye from across the street. I also like how you have the shop arranged. It's very cozy and inviting. Did you hire a professional to decorate your shop?"

The shopkeeper perked up and smiled. "I did it myself."

Words are important. The things you say can inspire, encourage, and uplift. They can be agents for harm or agents for healing. Speaking encouraging words doesn't take much effort, but it does take a conscious decision. Your choice to speak kind words will cause positive seeds of hope to be sown in the lives of others. Just like small seeds can grow into tall trees, those few kind words can provide shelter for someone in the midst of a storm.

Try this: Make an effort to listen to yourself. With a friend's approval, tape record yourself in ordinary conversation. Later, analyze the words that you chose and the way in which you used them. Be aware of anything that could be interpreted as offensive, and make conscious changes to speak words that will encourage, not discourage.

AN ANXIOUS HEART WEIGHS A MAN DOWN, BUT A KIND WORD CHEERS HIM UP.

PROVERBS 12:25 NIV

A PERSON'S WORDS CAN BE A SOURCE OF WISDOM, DEEP AS THE OCEAN, FRESH AS A FLOWING STREAM.

PROVERBS 18:4 GNT

Correction does much, but encouragement does more. Encouragement after censure is as the sun after a shower.

JOHANN WOLFGANG VON GOETHE

35

The Assignment

Commit to the LORD whatever you do, and your plans will succeed.

— *Proverbs 16:3 NIV*

Gwen wasn't happy making coffee. When she began her internship at the local news station, she imagined herself working with reporters, not cleaning up messes and taking lunch orders. After all, she wanted to be a reporter someday.

After just a couple weeks, a fellow intern quit and got a job in the mall. Gwen wondered if she should quit too. The work was unfulfilling, and she didn't think that she was making much of a difference. Gwen prayed, "God, I'm frustrated. Please show me what to do." God reminded her that learning was a process, and that if she stayed the course, she would be blessed.

A few weeks later, Gwen's boss called her into his office and asked if she would like to go on assignment with one of the reporters. Gwen couldn't believe the great news— finally a chance to cover a real story. When she was alone, she thanked God for helping her stay on track.

Have you ever been in a situation where you were asked to give your all and stay the course with no guarantee of payoff? If so, then you have probably learned that God won't put you in an impossible situation. Even if things didn't work out the way you hoped, you most likely learned from your experience and gained the satisfaction of knowing you kept your commitment. You should remember that most often your commitments will pay off. They are the containers that cradle your opportunities.

Try this: When you begin to feel unappreciated, examine your responsibilities. Seriously look for and list ways to do a better job and be more productive with your present duties. As you step out in faith, God will help you find those things that make your job more fulfilling. Don't worry about the future. God always rewards faithfulness.

Your hearts must be fully committed to the Lord our God.

1 Kings 8:61 NIV

Those who suffer according to God's will should commit themselves to their faithful Creator and continue to do good.

1 Peter 4:19 NIV

Stewardship is the acceptance from God of personal responsibility for all of life and life's affairs.

Roswell C. Long

God's Faithfulness

The withered flowers hold the seeds of promise,

The winter days are harbingers of spring;

The trials that may often seem most bitter

May bring to you the joys that make you sing.

Your roses may have thorns, but don't forget—

Your thorns may have some roses, too;

The Lord of great compassion loves you yet,

And He will never fail to see you through.

Author Unknown

Those who plan what is good find love and faithfulness.

— *Proverbs* 14:22 NIV

Through love and faithfulness sin is atoned for.

— *Proverbs* 16:6 NIV

GOD NEVER LEAVES. HE IS ALWAYS AT HAND AND IF HE CANNOT GET INTO YOUR LIFE, STILL HE IS NEVER FARTHER AWAY THAN THE DOOR.

MEISTER ECKHART

For Love's Sake

The fear of the LORD teaches a man wisdom,
and humility comes before honor.

~ Proverbs 15:33 NIV

Richard was one of those guys who didn't like to try anything he wasn't unusually good at doing. So when his son, Garrett, asked him to play in a father-son softball game, he balked. "Can't we play tennis or something?" Richard asked. "I'm not good at softball."

But ten-year-old Garrett was adamant. "Please, Dad, I really want to do this. It's only one game."

Richard agreed, but he wasn't happy about it. He remembered his less-than-stellar skills—missed catches, strikeouts, laughable throws. It seemed like a recipe for embarrassment, and on game day, Richard proved that his skills had not improved.

It didn't matter though. When Garrett enthusiastically introduced him to his friends, clapped loudly for Richard's one and only successful sprint to first base, and clung to his arm as they walked back to the car, Richard knew that humbling himself had paid a priceless dividend.

Richard could have held on to his pride and missed out on an important opportunity to bond with his son. God is pleased when you humble yourself for love's sake. He knows that you will soon be reaping a rich harvest of blessing both in your relationships with others and your relationship with him. If you have some area of pride in your life, let God show you how to break away and walk in the path of blessed humility.

TRY THIS: *Ask yourself where your prideful obstacles lie — we all have them. List them, which in itself is a humbling activity. Then ask God to give you opportunities to break through to blessings by humbling yourself in those areas. Remember: it's easy to miss humbling opportunities — your human self will want to brush them aside. Just keep your focus on the hidden treasure buried there.*

JESUS SAID, "WHOEVER HUMBLES HIMSELF LIKE THIS CHILD IS THE GREATEST IN THE KINGDOM OF HEAVEN."

MATTHEW 18:4 NIV

GOD GIVES GRACE TO THE HUMBLE.

PROVERBS 3:34 NIV

Humility is strong — not bold; quiet — not speechless; sure — not arrogant.

ESTELLE SMITH

Resting in the Lord

A heart at peace gives life to the body.

— *Proverbs 14:30 NIV*

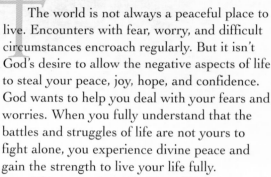

The world is not always a peaceful place to live. Encounters with fear, worry, and difficult circumstances encroach regularly. But it isn't God's desire to allow the negative aspects of life to steal your peace, joy, hope, and confidence. God wants to help you deal with your fears and worries. When you fully understand that the battles and struggles of life are not yours to fight alone, you experience divine peace and gain the strength to live your life fully.

This peace from God is unlike the natural peace you experience in your life. That type of peace fluctuates with circumstances. Divine peace is dependent on your relationship with God, and as long as you are living in close communion with him, it is a constant in your life, no matter what is going on around you. God's peace supernaturally calms your fears and serves as an assurance of his presence.

What a blessing!

Divine peace in your heart and mind is not subject to the whims of circumstance and fortune. It is a true and lasting peace that grows as you learn to trust God. If your life is filled with turmoil, ask God to fill you with divine peace. Your circumstances won't necessarily change, but you discover an inner confidence and know that God will be there to see you through whatever life has in store.

TRY THIS: *Practice keeping your thoughts under control. As thoughts of worry or doubt begin to creep in, make a conscious effort to focus your thinking on things that are good. On paper, assemble a list of these happy images (answered prayers, the love of those around you, blessings God has placed in your life). Add to your list regularly.*

WE HAVE PEACE WITH GOD THROUGH OUR LORD JESUS CHRIST, THROUGH WHOM WE HAVE GAINED ACCESS BY FAITH INTO THIS GRACE IN WHICH WE NOW STAND.

ROMANS 5:1–2 NIV

JESUS SAID, "I AM COME THAT THEY MIGHT HAVE LIFE, AND THAT THEY MIGHT HAVE IT MORE ABUNDANTLY."

JOHN 10:10 KJV

When thou hast Christ, thou art rich, and hast sufficient.

THOMAS À KEMPIS

What Would It Hurt?

Truthful witness does not deceive, but a false witness pours out lies.

~ *Proverbs 14:5 NIV*

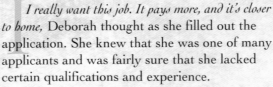

I really want this job. It pays more, and it's closer to home, Deborah thought as she filled out the application. She knew that she was one of many applicants and was fairly sure that she lacked certain qualifications and experience.

When she finished the application, Deborah looked it over disapprovingly. *Maybe I should rephrase this part,* she thought. *What would it hurt if I made this sound a little better?*

Deborah went back to work on her application, adding touches here and there. But as she indulged in small but significant exaggerations and embellishments, she heard God speaking softly but firmly to her heart, reminding her that he could not and would not bless dishonesty.

The next day, Deborah went back to her prospective place of employment. When the receptionist asked if her application was ready to submit, Deborah responded, "No, Ma'am. Could I have another blank application? It seems that I've made a mistake."

It's so easy to tell little lies, especially when they seem so harmless. You can try to justify them, but ultimately these small lies snowball into larger destructive forces. When you allow yourself temporary lapses in honesty, your integrity is compromised. If you justify telling small lies, you will eventually find yourself lying with greater frequency and less conviction. In time, deceit can become a part of who you are, with devastating consequences.

Try this: Use this two-step method to weed out dishonesty in your life. Whenever you catch yourself lying, ask God to forgive you and then apologize to the person you have attempted to deceive. This can be embarrassing and hard on the ego. But you will soon find yourself developing an "honest" habit.

A LIE HAS A SHORT LIFE, BUT TRUTH LIVES ON FOREVER.

PROVERBS 12:19 GNT

THE LORD DELIGHTS IN MEN WHO ARE TRUTHFUL.

PROVERBS 12:22 NIV

I consider the most enviable of all titles, the character of an honest man.

GEORGE WASHINGTON

TRUE TO GOD

Good people will be rewarded for their deeds.

~ *Proverbs 14:14 GNT*

It wasn't easy being far away from home, and life in the military proved difficult for a young Christian. Gina had only been in the service for one year, and had only been a Christian for six months before she was stationed overseas.

Having given her life to Christ, Gina turned away from her previous lifestyle. No longer did she give in to the impulses that once ruled her life. She felt like a new person and sought to live her new life in a way that would be pleasing to God.

Gina often found herself facing old temptations. She could have given up and given in. Instead, she relied on God's strength to see her through. She realized that without God's promises of help and the sense of his presence, she would never be able to remain true to her commitment. But with him by her side, she was able to remain faithful to him and continue to walk in the blessing her new life afforded.

Human beings are not perfect. None of us are capable of staying faithfully on the path of a godly lifestyle without God's help. That's the key. Because he is faithful to us, we are able to be faithful to him. When you face temptations, he is there. When you face discouragement, he is there. When you face hardship, he is there. He is always there providing just what you need to stay true to your godly lifestyle.

TRY THIS: *Like a detective, uncover the clues of God's providence in your life. Think about all the ways God has seen you through temptation, tough times, and difficult decisions. Write them down and keep them as encouragement to you to remain faithful. And don't hesitate to add to that list as you live your life God's way.*

THE FAITHFUL WILL ABOUND WITH BLESSINGS.

PROVERBS 28:20
NRSV

IF WE ARE FAITHLESS, GOD REMAINS FAITHFUL— FOR HE CANNOT DENY HIMSELF.

2 TIMOTHY 2:13
NRSV

Faithfulness and truth are the most sacred excellencies and endowments of the human mind.

CICERO

God's Family

I sought my soul—
But my soul I could not see;
I sought my God—
But my God eluded me;
I sought my brother—
And found all three.

Author Unknown

He who walks with the wise grows wise.

~ *Proverbs 13:20 NIV*

Jesus said, "Whosoever shall do the will of God, the same is my brother, and my sister, and mother.

~ *Mark 3:35 KJV*

CHRISTIAN BROTHERHOOD IS NOT AN IDEAL, BUT A DIVINE REALITY.

DIETRICH BONHOEFFER

On My Knees

When good people pray, the LORD listens.

— *Proverbs* 15:29 GNT

When Dwight hung up the phone, he wasn't sure what to do. He paced the floor of his barracks room, replaying the news in his mind. His dad had suffered a stroke and was in critical condition. Dwight wanted to be there, but being stationed overseas made that difficult.

Feeling helpless, he called a friend from church. When his friend arrived, Dwight explained what had happened. For the next twenty minutes, they prayed together on the floor of the barracks room. They prayed for Dwight's father's health, the welfare of the family, and Dwight's feelings of isolation.

When they finished praying, the outward circumstances seemed to be the same, but Dwight felt much better. He sensed God's presence, and he could think clearly. Through the rest of the night, Dwight stayed in prayer for his dad.

The next day, Dwight's company commander issued him emergency leave. Within twenty-four hours, Dwight was standing next to a hospital bed talking with his dad.

50

In Dwight's situation, confusion and fear were leading to frustration and feelings of isolation. Dwight had no control over the circumstances he was facing. But through prayer, God gave Dwight the assurance that he would see him through the crisis. Whenever you are unsure about what to do, it is a good rule of thumb to ask God. Through prayer, you can find answers that might otherwise be obscured by the emotional circumstances of the moment.

TRY THIS: *Associate prayer with every aspect of your life—working, eating, driving, or exercising. Keep a special journal, where you record those things you are praying about and God's answers. By nurturing a constant line of communication with God, you will feel God's peace descending even before you consciously ask.*

WHATEVER YOU ASK FOR IN PRAYER, BELIEVE THAT YOU HAVE RECEIVED IT, AND IT WILL BE YOURS.

MARK 11:24 NIV

THE LORD IS PLEASED WHEN GOOD PEOPLE PRAY.

PROVERBS 15:8 GNT

The purpose of all prayer is to find God's will and to make that will our prayer.

CATHERINE MARSHALL

Let's Go Fly a Kite

To do what is right and just is more acceptable to the
LORD than sacrifice.

— *Proverbs* 21:3 NIV

Steve promised his son, Ben, that he would help him fly his new kite over the weekend, but unexpectedly, Steve's softball team made the playoffs. The tournament scheduled Steve's team to play throughout Saturday and Sunday, leaving little time between games.

As Steve's team advanced through the playoffs on the first day, little Ben sat in the bleachers, waiting hopefully with his kite. The sun eventually went down in left field, ending any chance of kite flying for the day.

After church the next morning, Steve seated Ben in the bleachers once again. But it looked like kite flying would be edged out by softball just as before. The difference was that Steve had not forgotten his promise to Ben. At the end of the third inning, Steve spoke briefly with the coach in the dugout. The coach smiled and nodded. Moments later, Steve approached the bleachers.

"Son, let's go fly that kite of yours."

It is easy to get caught up in the moment and forget how the choices you make affect those around you. But when you take the time to consider the feelings of others, to keep your promises, to go out of your way to do what is right, that takes character. Steve realized how important it was to keep his word to Ben. Keeping your word is vital, especially when it comes to relationships. There is always someone watching, counting on you to do the right thing.

Try this: List the character traits you admire in others. Each week choose one of those traits. Write out the definition—look it up, even if you think you know what it means. Using the concordance in your Bible, find two verses that relate to that trait. Focus on that trait for the week, noting how well you measure up.

BLESSED ARE THEY WHO MAINTAIN JUSTICE, WHO CONSTANTLY DO WHAT IS RIGHT.

PSALM 106:3 NIV

THOSE WHO WALK UPRIGHTLY FEAR THE LORD.

PROVERBS 14:2 NRSV

The discipline of desire is the background of character.

JOHN LOCKE

Renewed Daily

Misfortune pursues the sinner, but prosperity is the reward of the righteous.

~ *Proverbs 13:21 NIV*

Nancy had been experimenting with drugs and alcohol. When her friends and family came together to confront her, she tearfully acknowledged that disaster awaited her at the end of that dangerous road. She asked God to forgive her and give her strength. And then with the encouragement of those who loved her, she set out to make important changes in her life.

God's forgiveness was immediate, but Nancy's desire to live a life pleasing to him required a daily renewal of her commitment. Walking away from drugs and alcohol was the most difficult thing she had ever faced.

As she stayed the course and sought God's help, Nancy began to glow with a divine beauty and live life with a quiet confidence. Her life could have been so tragically different. But Nancy made the decision to follow the path to life rather than death, to righteousness rather than despair.

Like Nancy and every other human being, you have a choice to make concerning the life God has given you. Taking the path that leads to righteousness and godliness will keep you on the road to blessing and right standing with God. Righteous living does not depend on your ability to live perfectly, only a determination to consistently choose, with God's help, those things that are right and good—and a willingness to ask for God's forgiveness when you do not.

Try this: *Each morning make a verbal commitment to live your day in a way that is pleasing to God. Then ask for his strength and discernment. In the evening before you go to sleep, ask God to forgive you for those times you have fallen short and to give you hope and courage to try again—with each bright new morning.*

In the way of righteousness there is life; along that path is immortality.

PROVERBS 12:28 NIV

Whoever pursues righteousness and kindness will find life and honor.

PROVERBS 21:21 NRSV

The most important ingredient of righteousness is to render to God the service and homage due to him.

JOHN CALVIN

55

It's an Attitude

The cheerful heart has a continual feast.

— *Proverbs 15:15 NIV*

A CHEERFUL
LOOK MAKES A
DISH A FEAST.
—GEORGE HERBERT

Cheerfulness is more than a perky personality trait. It's an attitude that causes you to see the best in other people and live with the expectation that good things will come into your life. It's an attitude that causes you to put aside negative thoughts and choose to give God the praise and glory for each new day.

True cheerfulness is an attitude that allows you to be compassionate, caring, kind, and encouraging to others no matter what your circumstances might dictate. Cheerfulness is in fact a sign of faith—that God will cause all things to work out for your good.

Cheerfulness and all the blessings that come with it are within your reach. Ask God to help you as you choose to see the positive side of life. Then ask him to help you spread that cheerfulness around through your smile and your happy disposition.

An attitude of cheerfulness is best maintained by choosing daily to put your life in God's hands. By so doing, you establish that your positive perspective on life is not dependent on the changing winds of circumstances. Instead, it is grounded in God, who is unchanging. Even during difficult times, see your attitude of cheerfulness as a sacrifice of praise to your loving Father. You will soon find that you can serve as a sign of hope and encouragement to others.

TRY THIS: *The next time that you feel disappointed or cheated in life, make a conscious decision to be cheerful. Force a smile and thank God for the good things he is doing for you. As your heart fills with cheer, the misery has nowhere to go, but out.*

A CHEERFUL HEART IS GOOD MEDICINE.

PROVERBS 17:22 NIV

A CHEERFUL LOOK BRINGS JOY TO THE HEART.

PROVERBS 15:30 NIV

Cheerfulness is among the most laudable virtues. It gains you the good will and friendship of others.

B. C. FORBES

God's Discipline

Oh, Lord, I present myself to Thee

Anything You require of me,

I am willing . . .

To receive what You give,

To lack what You withhold,

To relinquish what You take,

To surrender what You claim,

To suffer what You ordain,

To do what You command,

To wait—'til You say, "Go."

Author Unknown

Do not despise the LORD's discipline and do not resent his rebuke.

— *Proverbs 3:11 NIV*

He who heeds discipline shows the way to life.

— *Proverbs 10:17 NIV*

GOD DOES NOT DISCIPLINE US TO SUBDUE US, BUT TO CONDITION US FOR A LIFE OF USEFULNESS AND BLESSEDNESS.

BILLY GRAHAM

My Awesome God

Humility and fear of the LORD bring wealth and honor and life.

~ *Proverbs 22:4 NIV*

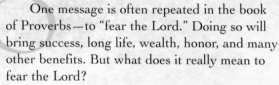

I FEAR GOD,
YET I AM NOT
AFRAID OF HIM.
—THOMAS
BROWNE

One message is often repeated in the book of Proverbs—to "fear the Lord." Doing so will bring success, long life, wealth, honor, and many other benefits. But what does it really mean to fear the Lord?

Fearing the Lord in this context means to hold him in highest esteem, to show him great respect, and to be in awe of his greatness. This is such an important concept because it places you in right standing with God and rightly aligns your relationship with him.

What could better ensure a happy and successful life than to see God for who he is and to rightly perceive where you are in regard to him? Fearing the Lord is the foundation, the cornerstone for all that is right and good in your life. It is surely the key that opens the doors of opportunity, blessing, wisdom, understanding, and success.

As you pursue success in your life and relationships, be sure to establish an attitude of respect and reverent awe for God. Such an attitude will take you to levels of achievement you would never be able to attain on your own. It will open your heart to his blessing and keep you on the right path. It will sustain you when you become weary and need to look to someone who is greater and stronger than yourself.

TRY THIS: *Each morning for one week, read a chapter from the book of Psalms. These beautiful songs are perfect representations of God in all his greatness and splendor. Before you read, ask God to begin to place within your heart a true sense of who he is and how you can relate to him as the wondrous creator of all that is.*

THE FEAR OF THE LORD IS THE BEGINNING OF KNOWLEDGE.

PROVERBS 1:7 NIV

FEAR THE LORD YOUR GOD, SERVE HIM ONLY.

DEUTERONOMY 6:13 NIV

It is only the fear of God that can deliver us from the fear of man.

JOHN WITHERSPOON

In Pursuit of the Goal

Apply your heart to instruction and your ears to words of knowledge.

— Proverbs 23:12 NIV

For two years, Cynthia had been carefully balancing her time between night classes at a local university and work. In pursuit of an education, she sacrificed much of her free time and, on occasion, a night's sleep. Sometimes she wondered if she would ever reach her goal to be the first person in her family to earn a college degree.

School had always been tough for Cynthia. Her grades were modest, and she knew she would never graduate with honors. But, deep down inside, Cynthia understood that her pursuit of learning was well worth the sacrifices she was making. She felt that a degree would not only help her professionally, but also improve her life skills and enhance her self-esteem.

It was difficult, sometimes downright discouraging, but Cynthia looked to God to help her continue to find joy in learning.

꧁ Is your personal comfort zone keeping you from branching out and learning something new? If so, you are doing yourself a disservice. Getting a college degree may not be one of your goals, but if you make it a point to find and take advantage of opportunities to learn, God will reward your efforts. And if you are looking, you will see those opportunities rising up to meet you. Your natural instinct may be to take the easy road, but God's way always leads to fulfillment.

꧁ Try this: *Make a list of things you would like to learn, and resolve to make them a reality. Take the top thing on the list and rough out how you could go about achieving that goal. Whether it's hitting the schoolbooks, learning a craft, or perfecting a particular skill, God will bless your brave endeavors.*

WISE STORE UP KNOWLEDGE.

PROVERBS 10:14 NIV

INTELLIGENT PEOPLE WANT TO LEARN.

PROVERBS 15:14 GNT

Learning is not attained by chance. It must be sought for with ardor and attended to with diligence.

ABIGAIL ADAMS

The Garden

Commit Whatever you do to the LORD, and your plans will succeed.

— Proverbs 16:3 NIV

WORK BECOMES
WORSHIP WHEN
DONE FOR THE
LORD.
—AUTHOR
UNKNOWN

Steve and Roberta decided to start a vegetable garden. They knew they couldn't use all the vegetables it would eventually produce, so they planned to share their harvest. Their garden would be dedicated to God.

Steve and Roberta soon discovered that the ideal of gardening and the reality of gardening were two different things. The work was hard. They had to till the ground and plant the seeds, but that was just the beginning. The garden also required constant watering, weeding, and mulching.

Despite the hours of hard work, Steve and Roberta continued to invest in the garden. As they watched the plants change from small, delicate sprouts to strong, sturdy plants, they felt a powerful sense of satisfaction. In time, beautiful vegetables were picked, cleaned, and given away. All their efforts became a blessing to others, a blessing to themselves, and an offering before God.

No matter what task you find before you, if you are willing to work hard you will receive God's blessing. It may involve physical labor or brain power. But if you offer your work to God and see it as your gift to him, you are sure to find satisfaction and enjoyment in your task. When your work is dedicated to God, it is he who will reward you with a sense of satisfaction. And it is he who will make your work a blessing to others.

TRY THIS: *Each time you begin a task, take time to commit your efforts to God. Ask for his guiding hand to be upon you as you strive to complete your task in a way that is pleasing to him. As you go about your work, imagine him right there at your side, working along with you. It will change the way you think about work forever.*

Hard work is a thrill and a joy when you are in the will of God.

ROBERT A. COOK

Give It to God

God guards the course of the just and protects the way of his faithful ones.

— *Proverbs 2:8* NIV

GOD'S MILL GRINDS SLOW, BUT SURE.
—GEORGE HERBERT

Denise had given her best to the company for eight long years. Now she was having trouble seeing the point. Three times in the past two months, her boss had taken her hard work and passed it off as his own. To make matters worse, he had given her a mediocre performance review.

A few of Denise's coworkers knew the truth, but they could do little to help. Denise felt that if she spoke up, she could end up in the unemployment line. Instead, she decided to plead her case before the Lord. Whether her boss's duplicity was exposed or not, she knew she would feel better and the Lord would see that justice was done.

Less than a month later, Denise's boss was fired—not for what he had done to Denise, but for lying to a client about his credentials—and she was asked to fill his position.

When you feel that you have been wronged, it is natural to want justice but wise to put your grievance in the hands of God. There will be times when you feel compelled to speak out on behalf of yourself and others. At other times, however, you may need to quietly entrust your case to God and wait for him to set things right. Waiting quietly for the Lord to act can be difficult, but in time, you will see that he is working within the situation and within hearts to bring a just resolution to your situation.

Try this: *The next time you suffer an injustice or encounter an unjust situation, tell the Lord all about it and briefly outline what happened in a notebook. At the top of the page, number the circumstance like this, "Case #1 presented to God on (today's date)." Ask God how you are to proceed, and don't act until you know with certainty what you should do.*

It is from the Lord that one gets justice.

Proverbs 29:26
NRSV

The Lord is known by his justice.

Psalm 9:16 NIV

Man is unjust, but God is just; and finally justice triumphs.

Henry Wadsworth Longfellow

God's Love

Love divine, all loves excelling,

Joy of heaven, to earth come down,

Fix in us Thy humble dwelling,

All Thy faithful mercies crown.

Jesus, Thou art all compassion.

Pure, unbounded love Thou art;

Visit us with Thy salvation,

Enter every trembling heart.

Charles Wesley

God is our God for ever and ever; he will be our guide even to the end.

~ *Psalm 48:14 NIV*

Beloved, since God loved us so much, we also ought to love one another.

~ *1 John 4:11 NRSV*

The love of God is like the Amazon River flowing down to water one daisy.

Author Unknown

Keep on Believing

There is surely a future hope for you, and your hope will not be cut off.
— *Proverbs 23:18* NIV

HOPE IS THE
PARENT OF
FAITH.
—C. A. BARTOL

Hope and faith work hand in hand. In fact, each is so much an integral part of the other, that it is easy to confuse them. Think of it this way—hope is the bottle God has given you in which to carry your faith. Or you could think of hope as the blueprint—a picture of what your faith promises to deliver one day.

While faith is rooted in belief, hope is rooted in desire. You begin with the desire, the hope, that God will work in your life. Then you use your faith to believe God will do just that. Since faith is a process, hope is needed to sustain you until the work is complete. Hope urges you on and encourages you to keep believing until God through faith has produced the very thing you are longing for.

Hope is the sense of expectation that washes over you as you read the Bible or spend time with God in prayer. It is the warm feeling of assurance you feel as you remember God's faithfulness in the past. It is the way your soul snaps to attention when someone comes to you with a word of encouragement. Hope is what sustains you as you wait for your faith to become substance. Embrace the hope God sends into your life and let it stimulate your faith that God will meet all your needs.

Try this: Each morning, ask God to fill your heart with hope and faith for the day ahead. As soon as you awaken, before you even get out of bed, close your eyes and see yourself going through the routines of your day—home, school, office—happily and successfully. Once hope has been established for that day, believe, by faith, that God will make it so.

SET ALL YOUR HOPE ON THE GRACE THAT JESUS CHRIST WILL BRING YOU WHEN HE IS REVEALED.

1 PETER 1:13 NRSV

A LONGING THAT IS MET IS LIKE A TREE OF LIFE.

PROVERBS 13:12 NIRV

What oxygen is to the lungs, such is hope for the meaning of life.

HEINRICH EMIL BRUNNER

LONGING FOR SOMETHING

The prospect of the righteous is joy.

~ *Proverbs* 10:28 NIV

JOY IS THE
SERIOUS
BUSINESS OF
HEAVEN.
—C. S. LEWIS

It seemed to Sarah that she was always longing for an illusive inner happiness, which seemed to be just outside her reach. Initially, she thought it would come in degrees as she achieved her goals: graduating from college, landing a good job. Those were happy times, but as the excitement of accomplishment faded, the happy, satisfied feelings on the inside faded as well.

Sarah then looked to her relationships to provide what she needed. That turned out to be a roller coaster ride. Sometimes her happiness barometer soared and sometimes it plummeted as people came in and went out of her life. Sarah then looked to money and possessions. They gave her a burst of happiness, but nothing sustainable.

It wasn't until she was invited to church one Sunday that Sarah found the answer. What she had been searching for was the constant, unconditional joy that comes from knowing God in a personal way. She found an inner happiness that never fades and never fails.

Many people confuse happiness and joy. Happiness is a temporary feeling of pleasure or contentment that fluctuates according to your outward circumstances. Buying a new car, for example, may make you happy, but when it breaks down, you aren't so happy any more. The Bible speaks of a permanent feeling of pleasure or contentment that emanates from within and is based in a person's relationship with God. The Bible refers to this as joy. It's never changing because God is never changing. It's one of the evidences of his presence in your life.

Try this: Take a look at your life. Does your sense of pleasure and contentment fluctuate with your circumstances? Or do you have a deep, inner sense of pleasure and contentment that flows out of a personal relationship with God? If you find that you possess mere happiness rather than joy, open your heart to a relationship with God. He's waiting with open arms.

THE PRECEPTS OF
THE LORD ARE
RIGHT, GIVING JOY
TO THE HEART.

PSALM 19:8 NIV

JESUS SAID, "MY
COMMAND IS THIS:
LOVE EACH OTHER
AS I HAVE
LOVED YOU."

JOHN 15:12 NIV

Joy is the most infallible sign of the presence of God.

LEON BLOY

Living in Wellness

Fear the LORD and turn away from evil. It will be a healing for your flesh and a refreshment for your body.

— Proverbs 3:7–8 NRSV

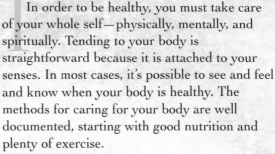

In order to be healthy, you must take care of your whole self—physically, mentally, and spiritually. Tending to your body is straightforward because it is attached to your senses. In most cases, it's possible to see and feel and know when your body is healthy. The methods for caring for your body are well documented, starting with good nutrition and plenty of exercise.

Your mind is more mysterious in its workings. It too needs a proper diet of good, uplifting thoughts and positive input. Exercise in the form of learning and inspiration are also needed in order to keep your mind fit and healthy.

Your spirit needs to be exercised with activities that strengthen your relationship with God, such activities as prayer, thanksgiving, and fellowship with people who know and love him. What about diet? Your spirit's food is the Bible. Each time you read and meditate on the scriptures, you are feeding and nourishing your spirit.

God wants you to be completely well so that he can accomplish all that he has planned to do in and through you. Do your part to keep yourself in good health physically, mentally, and spiritually by developing good habits in regard to diet and exercise. Let God show you what can be accomplished when the two of you work together toward a goal of total wellness. Consider it a way of honoring your Creator.

TRY THIS: *Keep a three-way record, documenting your physical health (weight, blood pressure, and other objective indicators), your mental health (stress level, moods), and your spiritual health (growing relationship with God). If you feel a little weak in any area, check out your diet and exercise routines.*

[GOD'S WORDS] ARE LIFE TO THOSE WHO FIND THEM. THEY ARE HEALTH TO YOUR WHOLE BODY.

PROVERBS 4:22 NIRV

JOHN WROTE, "I PRAY THAT EVERYTHING MAY GO WELL WITH YOU AND THAT YOU MAY BE IN GOOD HEALTH."

3 JOHN 2 GNT

God heals, and the doctor takes the fee.
BENJAMIN FRANKLIN

Knowing Him

The path of life leads upward for the wise.

— *Proverbs* 15:24 NIV

WHOEVER WALKS TOWARD GOD ONE CUBIT, GOD RUNS TOWARD HIM TWAIN.
—AUTHOR UNKNOWN

To Jerry, it seemed obvious that there was a God. No way could he believe the creation of the earth had been some amazing cosmic accident, an extraordinary collision of atomic particles, as some people said. What about all the creatures—intricate and diverse—how could they have evolved from a few fish? How could man be anything less than the creation of an intelligent benevolent God?

Jerry wasn't sure who God was, but he wanted to know. So he asked a friend.

"God is more than a cosmic innkeeper," his friend assured him. "I know him in a personal way, and you can too." Jerry's friend showed him in the pages of the Bible that God is a loving Father who cares deeply about each person. "He knows you intimately, completely," Jerry's friend continued. "And he wants you to know him. All he asks is that you open your heart to receive him."

The revelation of God in Jerry's life will take an eternity. But Jerry made the decision to begin, to reach out and take God's hand, to open his heart to know his love, his forgiveness, his compassion, his character. You can do the same. God loves you, and he has been waiting all your life for you to recognize your need to know him. Reach out and take his hand. Allow him to walk with you as you travel the path of life.

Try this: Find a quiet place, and focus completely on God who created you and all that is around you in the physical world. Ask him to be in your life—as a father, as a friend, as a counselor, as a provider, as the one who forgives all your sins and makes you clean and pure.

Until a man has found God, and been found by God, he begins at no beginning and works to no end.

H. G. Wells

God's Power

I sing the mighty power of God,
That made the mountains rise,
That spread the flowing seas abroad,
And built the lofty skies.

I sing the wisdom that ordained
The sun to rule the day;
The moon shines full at his command,
And all the stars obey.

Isaac Watts

There is no wisdom, no insight, no plan that can succeed against the LORD.

~ *Proverbs 21:30* NIV

The voice of the LORD is powerful; the voice of the LORD is full of majesty.

~ *Psalm 29:4* KJV

THE GOD OF THE BIBLE IS THE GOD WHO REVEALS HIMSELF IN ALL THE GLORY AND THE WONDER OF HIS MIRACULOUS, ETERNAL POWER.

M. LLOYD-JONES

79

Making Mistakes

He who conceals his sins does not prosper, but whosoever confesses and renounces them finds mercy.

— *Proverbs 28:13* NIV

Mercy is compassion in action.
—Author Unknown

Norman stared at the certificate of appreciation lying on his desk. When his boss had presented it to him for his important contributions to the company, he could barely believe it.

Just a week earlier, Norman discovered that a terrible error had been made in the pricing for a major sale—an error that cost the company more than $100,000. Worse of all, the mistake had been his.

Norman had gone straight to his boss's office and explained the details of the situation. Beads of sweat formed on his forehead as he waited for his boss's response. Norman expected to be fired, but it didn't happen—not that day and not in the week that followed. Together he and his boss planned a strategy to contain the damage and avoid future errors. Then to his surprise, he had been given the certificate. Norman knew that he had received mercy—from his boss and from God.

Mercy is a gift. It is about receiving something you don't deserve and not receiving what you do deserve. God poured out his mercy on humankind when he sent his Son, Jesus Christ, to pay the penalty for sin. Jesus is God's perfect son, but he gave himself freely to pay for the sins of others. Because he did so, you can now receive mercy rather than judgment, forgiveness rather than retribution. Reach out and receive his gift.

TRY THIS: Read the Bible story recorded in Matthew 18:21–35. This is a story that Jesus told his disciples to illustrate the concept of mercy. After you read it, ask God to make you aware of situations where you can show mercy to others as he has shown mercy to you.

JESUS SAID, "BLESSED ARE THE MERCIFUL, FOR THEY WILL RECEIVE MERCY."

MATTHEW 5:7 NRSV

BY MERCY AND TRUTH INIQUITY IS PURGED.

PROVERBS 16:6 KJV

We do pray for mercy; and that same prayer doth teach us all to render the deeds of mercy.

WILLIAM SHAKESPEARE

Being Known

A good name is more desirable than great riches;
to be esteemed is better than silver or gold.

~ *Proverbs* 22:1 NIV

CHARACTER IS
HIGHER THAN
INTELLECT.
—JEAN PAUL
RICHTER

After Clint opened a gas station in a small Midwestern town, he worked hard to gain the trust of the residents by always dealing honestly and fairly with them. With time, his customers learned to trust and respect him.

The station provided a good living for Clint and his family until, quite suddenly, gas prices dropped. Clint was concerned, especially when some of the bigger stations in town drastically lowered their prices in response. How could he continue to compete? He had already lowered his prices as much as he could afford to.

During that time, Clint was surprised and delighted to find that almost all of his regular clients continued to bring him their business. "Why do you keep coming here when gas is cheaper down the street?" he asked one of his customers. "We know you," the man answered. "You're an honest businessman who always provided good service and fair prices. Why would we go anywhere else?"

Building and keeping a good reputation is hard work. But once you have it, you will find that a good reputation is worth far more than you could have imagined. Not only will it see you through the tough times, like it did for Clint, but it will also enhance your relationships with others. A good reputation can even make you feel better about yourself by increasing your peace of mind and self-esteem. Never risk what you can't afford to lose.

Try this: Bring to mind an individual you have known who has a good reputation for being honest and fair. This might be a businessperson or someone else you know. Let him or her know that you respect and admire the reputation he or she has built. Briefly explain why someone should do this exercise. What are the benefits?

EVEN A CHILD IS KNOWN BY HIS DOINGS, WHETHER HIS WORK BE PURE, AND WHETHER IT BE RIGHT.

PROVERBS 20:11 KJV

A GOOD NAME IS BETTER THAN FINE PERFUME.

ECCLESIASTES 7:1 NIV

Glass, china, and reputation, are easily cracked and never well mended.
BENJAMIN FRANKLIN

Taking Care of Business

He who brings trouble on his family will inherit only wind.

— *Proverbs* 11:29 NIV

Gerald already worked a full-time job to support his wife, Doris, and their three children, but when his widowed mother required in-home nursing care that wasn't covered by insurance, he understood it was his responsibility to care for her. Gerald knew that God had entrusted to him the care of his family. He also knew that God would help him carry that responsibility if he were faithful.

To make ends meet, Gerald took on a part-time job and sold his fishing boat. He and his wife, Doris, agreed to cancel their vacation trip and tighten their budget in order to cover Gerald's mother's medical expenses. It was a tough time, but they were happy to do it.

Gerald's mother recovered slowly. It was almost two years before she could manage on her own again, but Gerald and Doris never regretted their decision to provide for her care. During that time, they realized more fully how much God loved and cared for them.

God is the architect of the first family unit, and within its boundaries he brought blessing and connectedness to the entire human race. Family is important to God, just as it should be important to you if you wish to live a life that is honoring to him. Even if you don't have a supportive, caring family, God's blessing will be upon you as you honor your responsibility to care for them.

TRY THIS: Do you have a family member with whom you have had a difficult relationship? If so, begin to pray daily for that person and your relationship with him or her. You will feel the blessing of God as he honors your willingness to do your part.

Family life is too intimate to be preserved by the spirit of justice. It can be sustained by a spirit of love which goes beyond justice.

REINHOLD NIEBUHR

Enough as Needed

A wise man has great power, and a man of knowledge increases strength.

~ Proverbs 24:5 NIV

When a man has no strength, if he leans on God, he becomes powerful.
—Dwight Moody

Tornado sirens echoed through the thunderstorm in the small farm town. Mary turned on the radio just in time to hear an urgent message that a tornado had touched down nearby. With her husband out of town on a business trip, Mary's heart raced. *I have to be strong*, she thought. *I can't let panic and confusion overtake me.*

Mary whispered a short prayer asking God for wisdom and strength. Then she sprang into action. She went upstairs and gently woke the kids. With a calm voice, she explained to the children what was happening. Holding hands, they all descended into the basement.

For the next thirty minutes, as the lights flickered, Mary kept the kids occupied with colorful stories from her childhood. After an hour, the storm passed. As she later tucked the kids back into bed, she thanked God for the timely strength he had given her.

In this life, from time to time you will encounter stressful, frightening situations that leave you fighting panic and confusion. God has given you a mighty provision. The next time you find yourself in one of those situations, don't become overwhelmed by fear and anxiety. God has promised to give you the strength you need to do what you have to do. Look to him. Not only will he fortify your own human strength, but he will infuse you with his divine strength. You will have all you need to see you through.

Try this: *Look up Philippians 4:13: "I can do all things through Christ which strengtheneth me." This is from the King James Version, but you can use any version you like. Write the verse on a card and if possible commit it to memory. Each time you find yourself in a frightening situation, repeat that verse over and over until you feel stronger.*

GOD GIVES STRENGTH TO THE WEARY AND INCREASES THE POWER OF THE WEAK.

ISAIAH 40:29 NIV

THE LORD SAID, "MY STRENGTH IS MADE PERFECT IN WEAKNESS."

2 CORINTHIANS 12:9 KJV

When God is our strength, it is strength indeed; when our strength is our own, it is only weakness.

SAINT AUGUSTINE OF HIPPO

God's Presence

Be thou a bright flame before me,

Be thou a guiding star above me,

Be thou a smooth path below me,

Be thou a kindly shepherd behind me,

Today, tonight, and forever.

Saint Columba of Iona

There is a friend who sticks closer than a brother.

~ *Proverbs 18:24* NIV

In my integrity uphold me and set me in your presence forever, O LORD.

~ *Psalm 41:12* NIV

GOD IS NOT AN IDEA, OR A DEFINITION THAT WE HAVE COMMITTED TO MEMORY, HE IS A PRESENCE WHICH WE EXPERIENCE IN OUR HEARTS.

LOUIS EVELY

I'm Listening

Plans fail for lack of counsel, but with many advisers they succeed.

~ Proverbs 15:22 NIV

Sally was proud of her new home-based business. She made a variety of homemade jellies and hoped to sell them at craft shows and county fairs. Sally worked hard making a great product, but after a few attempts at selling them, she became discouraged. She wasn't having much success, and she didn't know why.

After praying about the situation, Sally asked for the advice of a few friends who were successful small business owners. They all agreed that her jelly tasted great, but the packaging and presentation left a lot to be desired. They explained to her how creative marketing could attract more attention. Before the next fair, Sally took their advice and designed colorful labels for her jelly jars. In addition, she began giving out free samples. Before long, crowds of people gathered around her booth, anxious to get a taste. Her business was booming because she was willing to ask for the help she needed.

God wants you to succeed in all that he has given you to do. He has provided the help you need to make that happen by sending people into your life who can offer you wisdom, counsel, and good advice. Seeking out help can require a degree of humility, but it will pay huge dividends. Open up your heart and embrace the provision God has made for you. It is the surest path to success.

Try this: *Write a letter of thanks to three people who have offered you good advice and counsel in the past. Thank each person for the part he or she played in your success. This will inspire you to ask for help without hesitation the next time you need it.*

Listen to advice and accept instruction, and in the end you will be wise.

PROVERBS 19:20 NIV

He that hearkeneth unto counsel is wise.

PROVERBS 12:15 KJV

He that gives good advice, builds with one hand; he that gives good counsel and example, builds with both.

FRANCIS BACON

Right Moves

Good sense wins favor, but the way of the faithless is their ruin.

~ Proverbs 13:15 NRSV

Arriving at his son's little league baseball game, David couldn't believe his luck. He found a great parking space right next to the field. As David began walking toward the bleachers, he heard a voice. "It's not a good idea to park there." Dave looked over at an old man and replied, "What do you mean?" The old man went on to explain how foul balls have damaged cars in the past.

David thanked the man and found a new parking place. While watching the game, David saw others driving up and parking in the same place along the baseball field. As they got out of their cars, David saw the old man warning them of the same danger. Some heeded his warning, but most did not.

As the game progressed, David witnessed several foul balls that dented cars and cracked windshields in the exact area where he previously parked. He was glad he listened to the old man.

When David was confronted with a warning about where to park his car, he had a choice to make. Would he pay attention to what he had been told or take an unnecessary risk? Every day of your life, you have opportunities to make choices. It's up to you to use your good sense to make wise decisions. Life is uncertain enough. Why take unnecessary risks when you have the opportunity to do the smart thing?

Try this: When you are faced with a situation that requires a commonsense choice, hesitate long enough to consider the options. Then act only after you are satisfied that your choice makes good sense. This might seem inconvenient at first, but with time, you will find yourself responding more quickly to the situations around you.

Sensible people accept good advice.

Proverbs 10:8 GNT

Sensible people will see trouble coming and avoid it.

Proverbs 22:3 GNT

Truth is one of our simplest and most precious gifts. Without it we could not handle reality and negotiate life.

Os Guinness

A Confident Witness

The righteous are as bold as a lion.

— *Proverbs 28:1 NIV*

When Linda ate lunch with the ladies from her country club, she usually sat quietly and listened to their conversation. On one particular day, however, the topic of religion came up. As the women discussed their views on Christianity, Linda knew it was time for her to speak up. She politely put her dessert spoon down and began to recount her personal experience with Christ.

The women listened with interest and asked questions. Linda answered each one with insight and authority. Several of the women even sought her out later with more questions.

Linda was not by nature an outspoken person, but she learned something important that day. When she was willing to let God use her for his purposes, he provided the confidence and boldness she needed. As soon as she spoke the first word or took the first step, God reinforced, fortified, and strengthened her resolve.

Don't hesitate to be bold in your convictions, especially when it comes to your faith. The only way some people will ever know the truth about God is to hear it from you, from someone who knows him personally. Take every opportunity to share your beliefs, and look to God for the courage to speak boldly. Ask him for the right words and the ability to speak them kindly and effectively. You can be sure he will do his part as you do yours.

Try this: *Ask God to give you an opportunity to speak out about something you believe in strongly. Then watch carefully for opportunities to come your way. As you begin to speak, remember to do so gently and lovingly — no matter what the topic. You will soon feel God infusing you with boldness.*

My inmost being will rejoice when your lips speak what is right.

Proverbs 23:16 NIV

Since we have such a hope, [as glory], we are very bold.

2 Corinthians 3:12 NIV

Even a mouse can squeak with boldness when he stands on the shoulders of an elephant.

Dudley Adams

Leaning on the Lord

Trust in the LORD with all your heart and lean not on your own understanding.

— *Proverbs 3:5 NIV*

TRUST INVOLVES LETTING GO AND KNOWING GOD WILL CATCH YOU.

—JAMES DOBSON

When the company Karen worked for began to carry out budget cutbacks, she became worried and anxious. What would she do if the layoffs reached her desk? How would she make ends meet? Where would she find another position?

Karen's anxiety continued until one morning she remembered that she had failed to ask God for his help. As she opened the Bible and began to read, God spoke to her heart through the Scriptures. In Proverbs 29:25, she read: "The fear of man bringeth a snare: but whoso putteth his trust in the LORD shall be safe" (KJV).

Karen saw at once that her anxiety was rooted in fear—fear of what the company would decide. God wanted her to throw away her fear and put her trust in him. Peace filled her heart. Karen went to work that day knowing that no matter what the future held, she would get through it with God's help.

God never intended for you to be controlled by the uncertainties in your life. That's why he took so much care to let you know that you can place your trust in him. Throughout the Bible, his assurances shine forth. He doesn't promise that things will necessarily turn out as you expect them to. But he does say with certainty that he will take care of you in every situation you encounter. You won't have to face the circumstances of your life alone. God will be there to see you through.

TRY THIS: *Write out Proverbs 16:20 and Isaiah 12:2 on index cards and tape them to your bathroom mirror. Each morning as you prepare to face the day, read them out loud to remind you that God will be right by your side no matter what the day may hold. You will not be disappointed when you place your trust in him.*

HAPPY ARE THOSE WHO TRUST IN THE LORD.

PROVERBS 16:20
NRSV

SURELY GOD IS MY SALVATION; I WILL TRUST AND NOT BE AFRAID.

ISAIAH 12:2 NIV

He who trusts in himself is lost. He who trusts in God can do all things.
SAINT ALPHONSUS LIGUORI

God's Promises

God's promises are strong and true,
He backs them with his power.
Take them as you need them
For each day and hour.
Don't let worry wreck your life
As some are bound to do,
Take up the promises of God
And watch them work for you.

Andrea Garney

The name of the LORD is a strong tower; The righteous runs into it and is safe.

— *Proverbs* 18:10 NASB

I rejoice in your promise like one who finds great spoil.

— *Psalm* 119:162 NIV

GOD'S PROMISES ARE LIKE THE STARS; THE DARKER THE NIGHT THE BRIGHTER THEY SHINE.

DAVID NICHOLAS

Catching the Ball

You do yourself a favor when you are kind.

— *Proverbs* 11:17 GNT

Kindness is the golden chain by which society is bound together.
—Johann Wolfgang von Goethe

Allen loved everything about baseball. He had been going to the park with his dad since he was a boy. Twice through the years, he had known the wild excitement of catching a ball and taking home his prize. Though he was now a grown man, he still went to the park with his glove, ready to pick a misguided hit out of the air.

Tonight, early in the third inning, Allen's wait for catch number three seemed to be over as a batter sent the ball screaming in his direction. As some people jumped out of the way, others stretched forward, eager to take home a piece of the game. The ball was coming right to him when Allen glanced down and moved aside. The ball dropped into the glove of a young boy standing beside him. Allen grinned at the boy's excited whoops and bright smile.

An act of kindness is an investment in another person's life. It is an acknowledgment that other people are valuable and worthy to receive such a gesture simply because God created them in his own image. Reach out to someone today through a kind word or deed. Help your elderly neighbor up the steps with her bags, give a friend a ride, or offer someone a word of comfort or encouragement. The Bible says God's blessing will come to you when you do.

TRY THIS: *Keep a small notebook containing creative ways in which you can show kindness to others. As the ideas come to you, write them down with the expectation of putting them into action within fourteen days. Ask God to help you recognize opportunities as he places them in your path.*

BE KIND AND COMPASSIONATE TO ONE ANOTHER, FORGIVING EACH OTHER, JUST AS IN CHRIST GOD FORGAVE YOU.

EPHESIANS 4:32 NIV

ALWAYS TRY TO BE KIND TO EACH OTHER AND TO EVERYONE ELSE.

1 THESSALONIANS 5:15 NIV

One kind word can warm three winter months.

JAPANESE PROVERB

A Life Well Lived

The LORD is pleased with good people.

— Proverbs 12:2 GNT

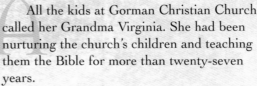

All the kids at Gorman Christian Church called her Grandma Virginia. She had been nurturing the church's children and teaching them the Bible for more than twenty-seven years.

Grandma Virginia genuinely loved each of the kids whose lives she touched, and they knew it. From her handmade sock puppets to her homemade oatmeal cookies, she dedicated her efforts to their spiritual and physical welfare. Even as she grew older, she rarely missed a Sunday morning. Grandma Virginia was well loved in her neighborhood as well, guiding those who could not be in her class on Sunday. Her arms were usually open with the promise of a much-needed hug, and her words were honest and wise.

One crisp fall morning, Grandma Virginia passed away in her sleep. She didn't leave much in the way of earthly belongings. Because of the rich goodness of her life, however, Grandma Virginia's legacy continues to affect those who knew her.

Anyone can and should engage in the doing of good deeds. The kind of consistent goodness that marked the life of Grandma Virginia is the result of an ever-deepening relationship with God. As you surrender yourself to him, his character begins to dominate your life more and more. What makes up God's character? Galatians 5 says that it consists of the following: love, joy, peace, patience, kindness, generosity, faithfulness, gentleness, and self-control. With God's help, you can live a life of goodness just as Grandma Virginia did.

Try this: *Give your heart a quick checkup. Ask yourself these questions and apply the answers to your daily life. How often do I do things for others? Do those actions glorify God? When others observe my life, what can they tell about my relationship with God? As you answer these questions, ask God to reveal the motives behind your actions.*

THOSE WHO PLAN GOOD FIND LOYALTY AND FAITHFULNESS.

PROVERBS 14:22
NRSV

THE GOOD PERSON OUT OF THE GOOD TREASURE OF THE HEART PRODUCES GOOD.

LUKE 6:45 NRSV

Goodness is easier to recognize than to define.

W. H. AUDEN

A Simple Misunderstanding

He who guards his lips guards his life.

— *Proverbs* 13:3 NIV

SPEAK IN A SPIRIT OF HUMILITY AND LOVE.
—BERNARD BONGLEY

Running late, Kate sped through the parking lot toward the office building where she worked, only to find an old van parked in her reserved parking space. Kate parked in the back of the lot and made her way through the rows of cars to the front door.

Kate entered the building and marched up to the security desk, ready to give someone—anyone—a piece of her mind. That's when she saw a stack of memos on the counter: REMINDER TO ALL THOSE USING RESERVED PARKING. The memo reminded tenants that the number of handicapped parking spots was being increased and the reserved parking area had been relocated to the west side of the building.

Kate felt a sheepish blush wash over her face. She had received a copy of that memo more than a week earlier. She had simply forgotten. As she walked away, she thanked God that she hadn't spouted off and made a fool of herself.

Once spoken, words cannot be taken back. That's all the more reason to make sure that your words are wise and purposeful. Resist the urge to speak rashly in times of intense emotion, such as anger, frustration, hurt, or even sympathy. Give yourself time to process your thoughts, choose your words, and express yourself clearly and effectively. When Jesus was here on earth, he always made his words count. He sent them out and they accomplished his Father's purpose. Ask God to help you make your words count.

Try this: *In Isaiah 55:11 (GNT), God says the following concerning his word: "It will not fail to do what I plan for it; it will do everything I send it to do." Write this verse on a card or commit it to memory. Ask God to help you model your words after his.*

A WORD APTLY SPOKEN IS LIKE APPLES OF GOLD IN SETTINGS OF SILVER.

PROVERBS 25:11 NIV

HE WHO HOLDS HIS TONGUE IS WISE.

PROVERBS 10:19 NIV

Be humble and gentle in your conversation; and of few words, I charge you; but always pertinent when you speak.

WILLIAM PENN

Catching Up

All hard work brings a profit, but mere talk leads only to poverty.

— *Proverbs 14:23 NIV*

"That's it! No more!" Lisa shouted. "I am sick of the stress of playing catch-up!" Lisa had always been a procrastinator, but now she was determined to do something about it.

Her car was in desperate need of an oil change. Her bills were always paid, but usually a few days late. Her refrigerator had at least ten items that were past their expiration dates—some of the items she didn't even recognize any more. On her desk were Christmas cards waiting to be mailed, although it was February. The accumulated stress from Lisa's procrastination was staggering. It seemed the more she got behind, the less likely she was to do anything to remedy the situation.

It is a tough transition, and Lisa still doesn't find disciplining herself easy. With God's help and the encouragement of her friends, she has begun to make steady progress. Every day she is able to enjoy a little more of the fruits of diligence.

Occasionally overlooking a small task or delaying an inevitable duty is no crime. But when procrastination becomes a way of life, trouble is always looking over your shoulder. It can strip you of your productivity, cause you to miss out on God's blessing, create embarrassing and often costly situations, and it can even rob you of God's best purposes for your life. If you struggle with procrastination, ask God to help you. Then do what you have to do: admit it and quit it.

Try this: Prioritize with a point system. Make a list of the things you need to accomplish in the next week. Assign points (1–10) to each task based on its importance and assign another number based on the urgency of the task. Add the two numbers together. Begin with the task with the highest point value and work your way down.

HARD WORK WILL GIVE YOU POWER.

PROVERBS 12:24 GNT

HANDS THAT WORK HARD BRING WEALTH TO YOU.

PROVERBS 10:4 NIRV

Putting off an easy thing makes it hard, and putting off a hard one makes it impossible.

GEORGE H. LORIMER

God's Provision

Thou that givest food to all flesh,

which feedst the young ravens

that cry unto thee

and hast nourished us

from our youth up:

fill our hearts with good and gladness

and establish our hearts

with thy grace.

Bishop Lancelot Andrews

The LORD does not let the righteous go hungry.

— *Proverbs* 10:3 NIV

God provides food for those who fear him; he remembers his covenant forever.

— *Psalm* 111:5 NIV

LABOR MAY
PROVIDE WAGES
THAT FEED THE
FAMILY, BUT GOD
IS ITS SOURCE.

DUDLEY ADAMS

Abiding Safely

He who fears the LORD has a secure fortress, and for his children it will be a refuge.

— *Proverbs 14:26 NIV*

My welfare is God's business, and business is good.
—Dudley Adams

As Margaret turned the corner into her neighborhood, she noticed what a beautiful day it was. The sun was shining, and everyone was outdoors enjoying the great weather. One of her neighbors was mowing near the street. Margaret had just lifted her hand to wave when she was startled by the sound of glass exploding.

Margaret stopped the car and looked behind her. A rock lay on the backseat surrounded by shards of broken glass. Her neighbor met her as she stepped out of the car. "I'm okay," she assured her neighbor as he apologized again and again. It was then that Margaret realized her neighbor's lawnmower had thrown the rock. If she had driven past only a split second later, the rock would have crashed through the driver's window. She would almost certainly have been injured.

Together, they carefully cleaned up the broken glass. As they worked, Margaret shared with her neighbor her confidence in God's ever-present protection.

God is looking out for you, even when you aren't aware of it. You may never know all the ways in which he protects you. In the Bible, he says that he commands his angels to guard you in all your ways (Psalm 91:11). What a marvelous promise. Thank God for his protective hand on your life, and the next time you find yourself in danger, remember he has marshaled the hosts of heaven to keep you safe.

TRY THIS: *Begin a policy of pre-praying. Pray for God's protection in advance. Pray each time you get in the car, whether you're taking a road trip or running an errand. Pray before you start working in the morning, before meals, and at bedtime. And don't hesitate to pre-thank God as well. This brief exercise will strengthen the lines of communication.*

THE LORD IS LIKE A STRONG TOWER, WHERE THE RIGHTEOUS CAN GO AND BE SAFE.

PROVERBS 18:10 GNT

GOD WILL KEEP YOU SAFE FROM ALL HIDDEN DANGERS.

PSALM 91:3 GNT

We sleep in peace in the arms of God, when we yield ourselves up to his Providence.

FRANÇOIS FÉNELON

Turning the Other Cheek

Do not say, "I'll pay you back for this wrong!" Wait for the LORD, and he will deliver you.

— *Proverbs 20:22 NIV*

> THE NOBLEST
> VENGEANCE IS
> TO FORGIVE.
> —HENRY G. BOHN

Nancy's list was almost complete, and the invitations were ready to be mailed. The list contained the names of the women she intended to invite to her Christmas party, but one name had been crossed out. Days before, Nancy had overheard this particular friend spreading an untrue story about her. In retaliation, she had removed her friend's name from the invitation list. *This will teach her,* Nancy thought to herself as she ripped up her invitation.

Now, standing in front of the mailbox double-checking the addresses on the holiday envelopes, she thought about the friend she had chosen not to include. *Not inviting her,* she thought, *will only make matters worse. Do I really want to lose her friendship completely? Would God be pleased with the way I'm handling this?*

Before the end of the day, Nancy made a new invitation for her friend and resolved to hand-deliver it.

Revenge is a lose-lose proposition. That's why God says not to engage in it no matter how severe the offense might be. There are no exceptions, making it clear that a wrong never justifies another wrong. It can't and won't change the circumstances. What it will do is drag you down to the level—morally, spiritually, emotionally—of the offender. When you've been wronged, leave your hurt and anger in the hands of God. Healing, justice, and reconciliation come from him.

TRY THIS: *Count the cost. When you are tempted to seek revenge, calculate what you stand to gain. Then, figure out what you stand to lose. Try putting the gains and losses down on paper. This will help you see that revenge doesn't solve problems, it multiplies them.*

"Do not seek revenge or bear a grudge against one of your people, but love your neighbor as yourself," says the Lord.

LEVITICUS 19:18 NIV

Do not repay anyone evil for evil.

ROMANS 12:17 NRSV

The only people with whom you should try to get even are those who have helped you.

JOHN E. SOUTHARD

You Have My Word

People who promise things that they never give are like clouds and wind that bring no rain.

— *Proverbs 25:14* GNT

He that promises too much means nothing.
—English Proverb

Chad couldn't believe it. More than a month earlier, he had promised a friend from work that he would help him move. He had forgotten all about his promise and made arrangements to go on a fishing trip.

When his friend dropped by his office to remind him, he visualized himself hauling furniture and boxes up three flights of stairs. Then he imagined himself relaxing out on the lake, a soft breeze blowing through his hair. No doubt about it, Chad would have preferred to be at the lake, but he knew God expected him to keep his word. Chad assured his friend that he would be there.

On moving day, Chad was the only one who showed up. This left more work for the two of them. Chad could imagine how badly his friend would have felt if no one had come. He whispered a prayer of thanks to God for urging him to keep his promise.

God has filled the Bible with promises—and he hasn't broken even one. If you wish to be like him, to follow his example, to please him, you must keep your promises too, without exception. The key to successfully keeping your promises is to watch your words carefully. Give thought and prayer to the promises you make. When promises are made, consider them a commitment to God as well as to another person.

TRY THIS: *Before you make a promise to anyone about anything, ask for time to check your schedule. If you feel it is a promise you're able to keep, write it on your calendar. To make sure you don't forget, add a reminder to the calendar a week before the date of your obligation.*

IT IS A TRAP FOR A MAN TO DEDICATE SOMETHING RASHLY AND ONLY LATER TO CONSIDER HIS VOWS.

PROVERBS 20:25 NIV

IN FRONT OF THOSE WHO RESPECT YOU, I WILL KEEP MY PROMISES.

PSALM 22:25 NIRV

Promises may get friends, but it is performance that must nurse and keep them.

OWEN FELTHAM

Winning God's Way

The horse is made ready for the day of battle, but victory rests with the LORD.

— *Proverbs 21:31 NIV*

As the time on the clock expired, a final gunshot marked the end of the fourth quarter and the conclusion to an exciting game. The numbers on the scoreboard told the tale. The home team had overwhelmingly won.

In a live television broadcast moments after the end of the game, a smiling player was interviewed amid a chaotic scene of celebration on the field. In the background, his teammates crowded around, eager to share their championship win with the TV viewers at home. Trying to be heard over the voices of cheering fans, the reporter leaned in and asked the player how he was able to lead his team to victory. Before the game's hero explained any specific strategies or game plans, he looked directly into the camera and said, "I want to thank God because none of this would have been possible without him."

God is completely just. He doesn't provide an unfair advantage for one team over another. So what did the football player mean when he said that God made the home team's victory possible? He meant that God invested gifts and talents in the lives of the players. He meant that God gave those players opportunities to develop their gifts into well-honed skills. He was acknowledging that God motivated the team members to do their best. That's a winning formula.

TRY THIS: *Make a list of the gifts God has placed in your life—things like playing the piano, running track, drawing pictures, writing, organizing people, making people laugh. Then choose three, and ask yourself what you're doing to become skillful in those areas. Ask God to help you plan a strategy for becoming a winner in regard to each one.*

GOD HOLDS VICTORY IN STORE FOR THE UPRIGHT.

PROVERBS 2:7 NIV

THANKS BE TO GOD! HE GIVES US THE VICTORY THROUGH OUR LORD JESUS CHRIST.

I CORINTHIANS 15:57 NIV

Spiritual victory comes only to those who are prepared for battle.

AUTHOR UNKNOWN

God's Will

Whate'er God will, let that be done'

His will is ever wisest:

His grace will all thy hope outrun.

Who to that faith arisest,

The gracious Lord, will help afford'

He chastens with forbearing:

Who God believes and to him cleaves,

Shall not be left despairing.

Albrecht of

Brandenburg

All our steps are ordered by the LORD.

— *Proverbs 20:24 NRSV*

Do not be foolish, but understand what the will of the Lord is.

— *Ephesians 5:17 NRSV*

Inside the will of God there is no failure. Outside the will of God there is no success.

Benard Edinger

PURE OF HEART

The lamp of the LORD searches the spirit of a man; it searches out his inmost being.

— *Proverbs 20:27 NIV*

MAN SEES YOUR
ACTIONS, BUT
GOD YOUR
MOTIVES.
—THOMAS À KEMPIS

When Jared decided to go after the third district city council seat, he campaigned hard. The people from the strongly conservative neighborhood received him well. As the son of a local clergyman, he often spoke in area churches relating his commitment to God and assuring the voters that he would make godly decisions on their behalf.

The voters loved him and gave him the council seat by a wide margin. He had used the right words, told the right stories, and espoused the right issues. He had pulled it off.

But God was not fooled. He looked beyond Jared's words and actions. He looked straight into Jared's heart. There he saw a different picture—one of a man with a thirst for power and strong ambitions that did not include a relationship with God. God knew the truth about Jared's motives. By the time the next election came around, so did the people of the third district.

Most people see only what you want them to see—the words, actions, and surface emotions displayed in your life. It's easy enough to hide your true motives from them. The eyes of God look much deeper. They identify the motivations behind the things you do. They see into your heart. To please God, you must be as pure on the inside as you appear to be on the outside. If you aren't proud of your inner motives, ask him to forgive you and help you set things straight.

TRY THIS: *The next time you decide to do something that looks good on the outside, ask God to show you your true motive. It could be that you find yourself enjoying a harvest of inner godliness. If you find a weed of selfish ambition, ask God to root it out. Then go ahead and do the good thing for the right reason.*

Pure motives will make a clear flame. Impure motives are the smoke that clogs the flame.

SIDNEY COOK

A Transformed Mind

The LORD detests the thoughts of the wicked, but those of the pure are pleasing to him.

~ Proverbs 15:26 NIV

OUR LIFE IS
WHAT OUR
THOUGHTS
MAKE IT.
—SAINT CATHERINE
OF SIENA

As long as she could remember, Samantha had struggled with negative thinking. These dark thoughts left her dissatisfied and unhappy. But when Samantha gave her life to God, many things began to change.

Samantha discovered that she had been allowing her mind to linger unchecked. Whether her thoughts had been based in fear, jealousy, or despair, Samantha pulled them in close and made them her own. Now she learned that God wanted her to release those negative thoughts to him and allow him to replace them with good, encouraging thoughts.

Samantha's path to victory over her negative thoughts was a difficult one. It meant studying the Bible, God's Word, along with the help of a capable, godly teacher. It also took a commitment to prayer, and the support of her family and close friends. It wasn't easy, but as Samantha was faithful to do her part, God was faithful to do his.

122

In Philippians 4:8, God urges Christians to focus their thoughts on things that are true, noble, right, pure, lovely, admirable, excellent, and praiseworthy. That is an ambitious goal that cannot be achieved without his help. If you are struggling with unproductive, destructive thoughts, ask God to help you practice the pattern for good thinking outlined in Philippians. If you let him, God will help you transform your mind, one thought at a time.

TRY THIS: *Prompt yourself with thinking points. On 3 x 5 index cards, make a list of specific things in your life that are genuinely pure and lovely—friends, fellowship, blessings, and your relationship with God, for example. Be as specific as possible. When you are assailed by negative thoughts, use these thinking points to regain control. Once a week, create a new list.*

THE LORD KNOWS WHAT PEOPLE THINK. HE KNOWS THEIR THOUGHTS.

PSALM 94:11 NIRV

THE THOUGHTS OF THE RIGHTEOUS ARE RIGHT.

PROVERBS 12:5 KJV

Occupy your minds with good thoughts, or the enemy will fill them with bad ones.

SIR THOMAS MORE

God's Word

The Spirit breathes upon the Word,

And brings the truth to light;

Precepts and promises afford

A sanctifying sight.

A glory gilds the sacred page,

Majestic like the sun;

It gives a light to ev'ry age,

It gives, but borrows none.

William Cowper

Every word of God is flawless.

— *Proverbs 30:5* NIV

The word of God is quick, and powerful, and sharper than any twoedged sword.

— *Hebrews 4:12* KJV

THE WORDS OF GOD, WHICH YOU RECEIVE BY YOUR EAR, HOLD FAST IN YOUR HEART.

POPE SAINT GREGORY I

Other books in the Proverbs for Life™ series:

Proverbs for Life™ for Men
Proverbs for Life™ for Teens
Proverbs for Life™ for Women

All available from your favorite bookstore.
We would like to hear from you.
Please send your comments about this book to:

Inspirio™, the gift group of Zondervan
Attn: Product Development
Grand Rapids, Michigan 49530

www.inspirio.com

<u>Our mission:</u>
To provide distinctively Christian gifts that point people to God's Word
through refreshing messages and innovative designs.

inspirio™

The gift group of Zondervan